Ping Pong Face

乒乓脸

Yau Ming Ng-Thompson 吴友明/ 著

Illustrated by Andrés J. Colmenares

安德烈斯 • 科梅纳雷斯/ 图

For Ian, Sean, and all ping pong lovers.
献给延汉，蒜和喜爱打乒乓的朋友。

版权所有 不准翻印

ISBN-13: 978-0692087398
ISBN-10: 0692087397

Ping Pong
乒乓脸
Pong
Face

Yau Ming Ng-Thompson 吴友明/ 著

Illustrated by Andrés J. Colmenares

安德烈斯 • 科梅纳雷斯/ 图

Daddy slowly serves the first ping pong ball to Ian.
爸爸缓慢地发第一粒乒乓球给延汉。

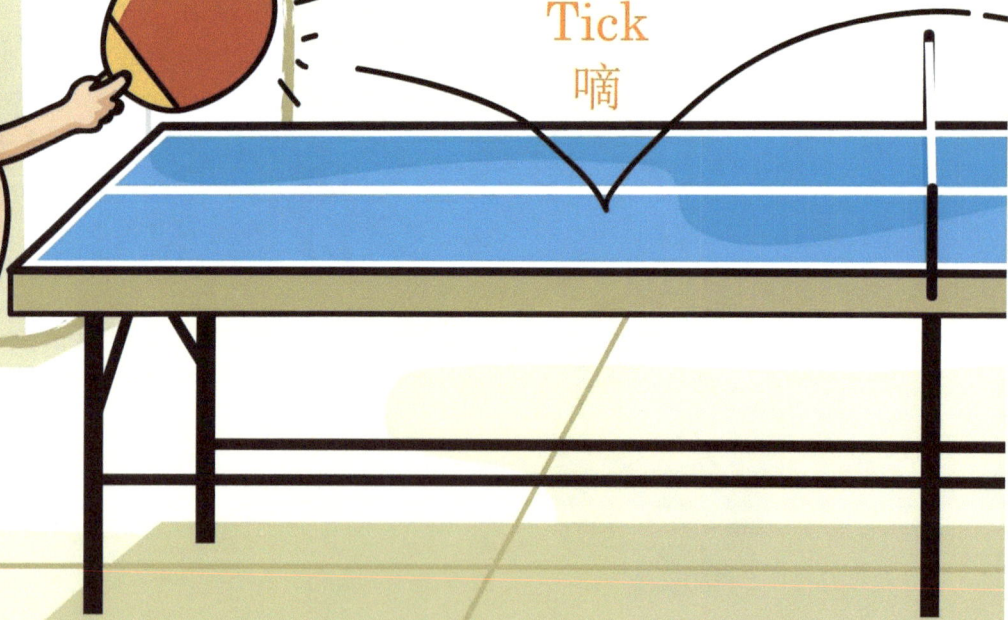

Tick
嘀

Tock
嗒

Ian swings his paddle hard, but he misses the ball.
延汉奋力的挥动球拍，但他接不到球。

Tick
嘀

Daddy gently serves the second
ping pong ball to Ian.
爸爸轻轻地发第二粒乒乓球给延汉。

Tock 嗒

Ian swings his paddle harder,
but he misses hitting the ball again.
延汉更加卖力地挥动球拍，但他再次接不到球。

Tick
嘀

Tock
嗒

Daddy softly serves
the third ball.
Ian misses the ball
once more.

爸爸缓和地发第三球。延汉再次失误。

Ian is getting frustrated. He starts to pout and complain.

延汉感到沮丧。他噘起小嘴，开始抱怨。

"Daddy, this is too hard. I don't want to play anymore."

"爸爸，这太难了。我不要再玩了。"

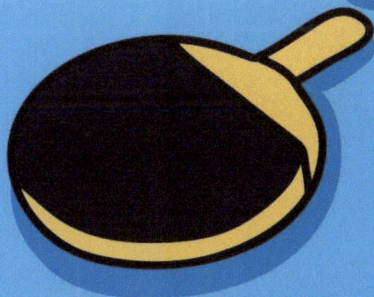

"How about you serve the ball to me?" Daddy asks.

爸爸问："那你试着把球发给我好不好？"

"Okay," Ian says.
延汉说："好吧。"

Ian positions himself to serve the ball to Daddy.
延汉摆好姿势准备发球给爸爸。

Ian misses the ball, hitting the table instead.
延汉挥拍落空，球拍击碰到球桌上。

Smack!
啪！

Ian tries to serve again.
延汉试图再次发球。

He swings his paddle
and hits the ball this time.
But the ball flies over and
across the table, hitting the garage wall.
这次他挥动着球拍，击中了球。但是球飞过桌面，撞上了车库的墙壁。

Ian starts to complain again.
"Daddy, this is too hard. I can't do it."
延汉又开始抱怨了。
"爸爸，这太难了。我做不到。"

Ian pouts. He is ready to give up.
<u>延汉</u>噘起小嘴, 他准备放弃了。

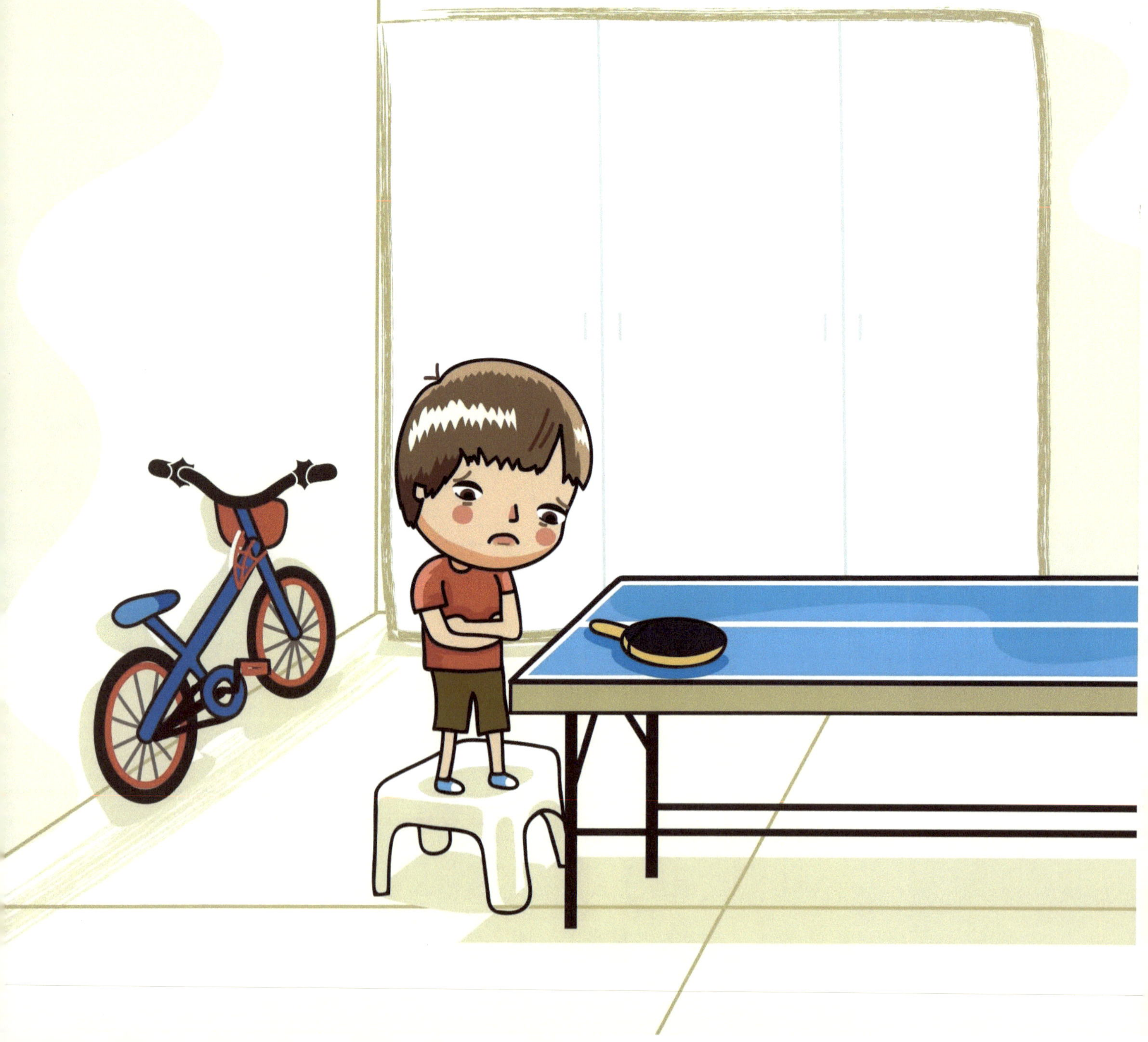

"Ian, slow down," Daddy says.
"Try to focus. I will give you a sticker if you hit or serve a ball correctly."
爸爸说："延汉，慢下来一点儿，专注一些。如果你击中或发对一球的话，我就给你一张贴纸。"

Ian thinks to himself, "If I get twenty more stickers, I can get the Lego set that I want."
延汉暗自衡量着："如果我再取得二十张贴纸，我就可以得到我想要的乐高组装玩具了。"

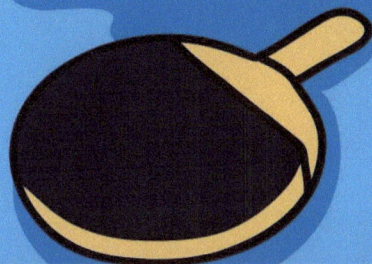

Ian has helped with house cleaning,
在这之前，延汉通过帮忙清理房子，

car washing,
洗车

and shoe shining,
和擦皮鞋，

has daily read a few pages of a book,
及每天阅读几页书藉，

and has even counted from one hundred to one
to earn the eighty stickers he has so far.
还要从一百倒数到一来赚取那八十张贴纸。

100, 99, 98, 97,
96, 95, 94, 93,
92, 91, 90, 89...

If he can only get those last twenty stickers!
只要他可以再次赢取那最后的二十张贴纸！

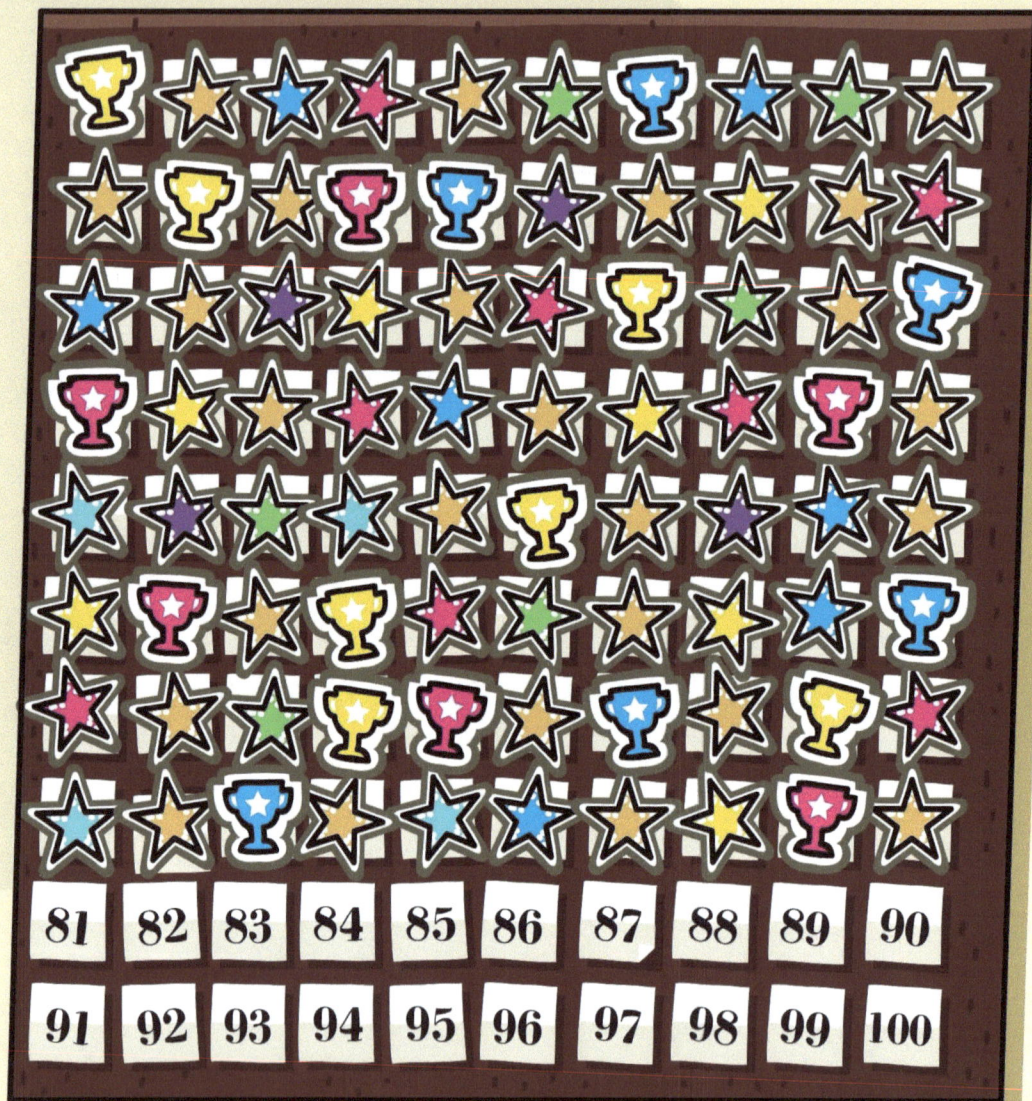

| 81 | 82 | 83 | 84 | 85 | 86 | 87 | 88 | 89 | 90 |
| 91 | 92 | 93 | 94 | 95 | 96 | 97 | 98 | 99 | 100 |

Ian has an idea.
<u>延汉</u>有一个主意。

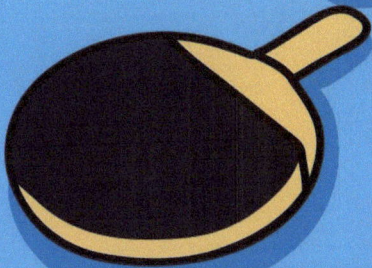

"Daddy, how about three stickers instead?"
"爸爸，给我三张贴纸吧？"

Daddy smiles at his little bargainer and agrees.
爸爸点头微笑答应了这个小小交易。

Ian focuses really hard. He squints his eyes.
He puts on a serious face and says,
"I'm ready, Daddy."
延汉用专注锐利的眼神, 很严肃地说:
"爸爸, 我准备好了。"

Daddy gently serves a ball to Ian.
爸爸轻轻地发一球给延汉。

Ian hits the ball with his paddle.
延汉用球拍击中了球。

Dock
哚

The ball lands on Daddy's side
of the table as it's supposed to.
球落在爸爸的桌面上，准确无误。

Tock
嗒

Daddy is stunned !
爸爸惊呆了！

He serves another ball.
他再发另一球。

Tick
嘀

Ian returns the ball perfectly again.
延汉又完美地回击了一球。

Dock
哚

Tock
嗒

Daddy serves a third ball.
爸爸再发第三球。

Dock
哚

Tock
嗒

And Ian hits it again and then again, making it five times in a row.
延汉再次准确的击中它，总共连续完美地回击五球。

Daddy is very impressed.
爸爸为孩子感到自豪。

Ian is so proud of himself.
延汉也为自己感到骄傲。

But getting too proud makes Ian lose focus. He starts to miss balls again.

但是骄傲让延汉分散了注意力。
他又开始失误了。

Tock
嗒

Tick
嘀

"Put on your ping pong face, Ian,"
Daddy reminds him. "Focus!"

"延汉，套上你的乒乓脸。"爸爸提醒他："专注!"

Ian focuses hard and squints as he puts on
a very serious face again.
延汉再次表现得非常严肃，全神贯注起来。

Ian decides to serve a ball. The ball bounces on his side of the table – tick –

这次延汉决定发球。球在桌子上跳动 – 嘀 –

Tick

嘀

and bounces on Daddy's side of the table – tock.
然后反弹在爸爸的
桌面上－嗒。

Tock
嗒

Daddy is stunned. "Wow!" he says.
"Impressive! Good job, Ian."
爸爸惊呆了。"哇！太棒了！干得好，<u>延汉</u>！"

Ian is happy.
延汉很开心。

He tries to serve a ball again to Daddy.

他再次试图发球给爸爸。

Tick
嘀

And he does it right again,
making it another two serves in a row!
他连续发了两粒好球！

Tick
嘀

Tock
嗒

Ian is super happy. Not only has he earned the stickers he needs for his Lego set,

延汉非常高兴。他不但赢取了乐高组装玩具所需的贴纸，

but he has learned that sometimes he has
to slow down and focus to make things
work.

而且他还了解到 -- 有时候他必
须放慢脚步和专注才能把事情
做得好。

Thank you for reading *Ping Pong Face*, my second children's book. I love reading and writing children's stories so much that I would trade my beauty sleep for writing! If you like this book, please share it with others by taking a few minutes to write a short review on Amazon. You may also enjoy my first book, *Three Going On Ten*.

Thank you,
Yau Ming Ng-Thompson

感谢您阅读我的第二本儿童书—《乒乓脸》。我喜爱阅读和撰写儿童故事，有时候我宁愿熬夜不眠来写稿呢! 如果您喜欢此书，请花数分钟的时间于亚马逊网页写下您的感言或评语与大家分享。您也许会喜欢我的第一本作品 — 《三期盼十》。

在此我也趁这个机会来谢谢帮我译校的朋友们— 简宝苹，黄嘉玲，陈玉莲和黄睬琍。

谢谢大家!
吴友明

www.ingramcontent.com/pod-product-compliance
Lightning Source LLC
Chambersburg PA
CBHW041545040426
42447CB00002B/56